GETTING THE MOST OUT OF
MAKERSPACES
TO GO FROM
IDEA TO MARKET

THERESE SHEA

ROSEN
PUBLISHING®

New York

Published in 2015 by The Rosen Publishing Group, Inc.
29 East 21st Street, New York, NY 10010

Library of Congress Cataloging-in-Publication Data

Getting the most out of makerspaces to go from idea to market/Therese Shea.—
First edition.
    pages cm.—(Makerspaces)
Includes bibliographical references and index.
ISBN 978-1-4777-7795-4 (library bound)—ISBN 978-1-4777-7797-8 (pbk.)—
ISBN 978-1-4777-7798-5 (6-pack)
1. New products—Juvenile literature. 2. Inventions—Juvenile literature. 3. Product design—Juvenile literature. I. Title.
TS170.S54 2015
658.5'752—dc23

                                                                    2014001216

Manufactured in the United States of America

CONTENTS

INTROD

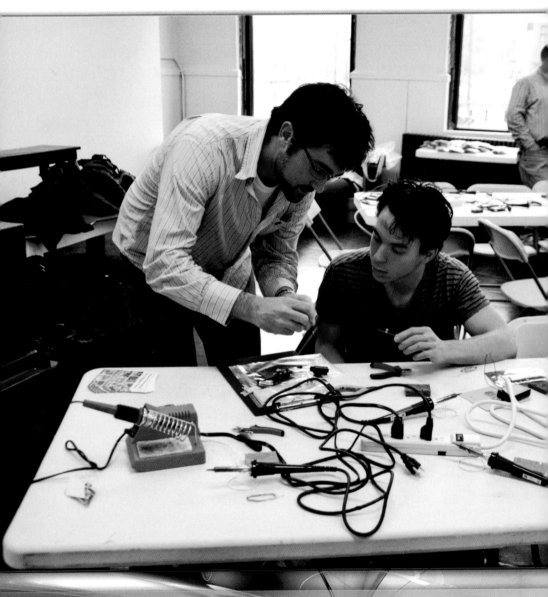

Makerspaces provide tools as well as the opportunity to work with people who have the knowledge and experience to help others succeed with projects.

Have you ever heard of a makerspace? What about a hackerspace, hacklab, hackspace, fablab, or tech-space? Though some would argue that each has a differ-ent focus, most would agree that they are basically the same thing. A makerspace is any place in a community with tools and supplies that enable individuals—called makers—to learn, create, invent, network, and share skills and knowledge. To be a maker, a person does not need a degree from a technical college or years of experience tinkering with computers. All one needs is interest.

While makerspaces might sound like a recent devel-opment, they are not. Early makerspaces did not house the large amount of tools that many have today, however. Instead, these first spaces often focused on the teaching of certain skills. Perhaps not surprisingly, some of the first makerspaces were libraries, which traditionally have been places to learn. Libraries still host makerspaces today, as do community centers, colleges and universities, and private businesses.

Makerspaces are for anyone with an idea. Today's makerspaces are often for all age groups. They are for children learning to construct robots, teenagers putting together a computer from parts, and adults working on home-improvement projects. Anyone can be a maker, and makerspaces are making it possible for anyone to be an inventor, too. In fact, they are leveling the playing field of entrepreneurship.

What is entrepreneurship? It is the ability and willingness to develop, organize, and manage a business venture, as well as assume the risks that go along with that. An entrepreneur must be prepared to invest a certain amount of money that he or she may lose if the business does not succeed. Many entrepreneurs begin with an idea for a product, an invention that they believe others will want to invest in. While this is fine for people with connections to the business world or those with enough money and resources to begin production, bringing a product to market is a scary prospect for most people. It is especially difficult for many young people to know where to turn if they want their idea to become a reality, even just one prototype. Most lack the money and resources.

This is where makerspaces come in. They have tools, machines, and materials that an inventor might need—some common and some quite specialized and expensive. They also have people to teach makers how to use these things and offer feedback on projects so that they can be tweaked to perfection. All of this is available for free or at a reasonable cost. Some makerspaces even offer guidance on how makers can take their product to market, a sometimes confusing and frustrating process.

Makerspaces have become very popular in the past few years. The increasing number of spaces and enthusiastic users have been called the "makerspace movement." Whether a maker is just in it for the fun of figuring out how to do something or is focused on creating the "next big thing," makerspaces are ready and waiting.

CHAPTER ONE
INVITATION TO INVENT

When Jason Perkins joined a Baltimore, Maryland, makerspace, he was primarily interested in learning about CNC machining. However, just a month later, he had developed the skills to build a prototype of a speaker system that combined technologies such as Bluetooth and Wi-Fi. Perkins decided to bring his product to market and manufacture for others what he called the Tubecore. He successfully raised enough money on the Internet to buy the parts needed to begin producing audio systems for a profit.

According to the *Baltimore Sun*, Perkins sold more than one hundred Tubecore systems in eight days, each retailing for up to $400. His invention has been praised in many technology magazines, including *Wired*. Even Perkins was surprised by his success, which he freely admits he owes to Baltimore Hackerspace. On the space's official website, Perkins is quoted as saying: "All in all, I never could have finished this project without the space." Perkins' makerspace embodies the makerspace ideal. It is a place for "socializing, learning, collaborating, and building…Each member has their own strengths and as a group [they] can accomplish anything." They can even accomplish beginning a successful business!

Besides filling the need for a place for people to share knowledge and create, makerspaces also present opportunities that many, like Jason Perkins, might never have. They are providing technology and experience that are only accessible in

A boy tries out energy-producing wheels in Vancouver, Canada. Maker Faires and Mini Maker Faires, like this one, are increasing interest in makerspaces.

certain manufacturing or collaborative environments. Where and when did these places come about?

BORN IN EUROPE

The first modern makerspaces were born in Europe. The hacker culture drove the birth of the spaces, providing a place for people to experiment with computers, software, programming, and other types of technology. Some were secretive organizations, setting up in abandoned buildings, while others were public, requiring membership fees and donations to keep them running.

Another called c-base began around 1995 in Berlin, Germany, and is often credited as the first modern makerspace. Like many of the early modern makerspaces, it is home to hackers, science-fiction enthusiasts, and digital artists. The building in which its members meet reflects this: it looks like a spaceship. Members have continued the myth that it is actually a spaceship that crashed long ago. In fact, when nonmembers enter restricted rooms, an alarm blasts the warning, "Alien! Alien!" C-base operates as a democracy, with all members voting on issues every two weeks.

Metalab in Vienna, Austria—established in 2006—is thought to have inspired the model of many makerspaces today. Though it has a governing board and paying members, it invites everyone to participate in whatever activities are taking place. Instead of keeping the club closed to the public, it invites the expert, the hobbyist, and the just curious to check out what is going on. Metalab assumes that enough people

HACKING: GOOD OR BAD?

Makerspaces that call themselves hackerspaces, such as Baltimore Hackerspace, use the word in the constructive sense. Historically, the word "hack" has had both positive and negative meanings. At first, hacking meant cleverly engaging in technical work. It came to mean gaining unauthorized access into technical and computer systems in order to understand how things work. Hackers became most famous for "breaking in" to these systems for illegal purposes, especially with

The Gainesville Hackerspace of Florida uses the word "hacker" in the positive sense. Its members promote creativity and ingenuity.

the advent of the Internet. That is why, in a *Make* magazine article, *Make*'s founder, Dale Dougherty, said he was originally going to call his magazine *Hack* but allowed his daughter to convince him that the title *Make* was the better choice.

However, hacking also came to mean manipulating either electronic devices or other machines to work in an unintended way. It meant making such devices one's own. In this way, hacking took on a positive meaning again. In a Wired.com article, Nick Farr, the founder of HacDC, said part of the reason for establishing his space was "to show people that hackers aren't criminals, that they're creative types."

will like what they see and want to become members to help support it. So far, this system has worked.

FIRST U.S. MAKERSPACES

Make magazine has been credited as one of the vehicles for the American maker movement. First published in 2005, *Make* registered the Internet domain name makerspace.com. It helped popularize the term "makerspace," using it to encompass all public spaces where people create and design. The term better reflects the diversity of many makerspaces today, underscoring the idea that they are not just for computer hackers and technical wizards.

According to *Make* magazine, TechShop, a for-profit chain of spaces, opened in California beginning in 2006. TechShop calls itself "America's First Nationwide Open-Access Public Workshop." The chain provides access to woodworking, machining, welding, sewing, and CNC fabrication tools and equipment for a fee.

HacDC of Washington, D.C., is a nonprofit makerspace that opened in 2007. The group's founder, Nick Farr, opened it after visiting c-base in Germany. On his space's website, Farr said he wanted "to build a place where people could work on their projects, have a good time and get others involved in art, technology and service."

FIRST LIBRARY MAKERSPACES

C-base may have been the first modern makerspace, but the first library makerspace formed in 1873, according to an article in the *American Libraries Magazine*. A library in Gowanda, New York, recorded becoming a place where a ladies society met to quilt, sew, knit, and talk about books. Later, libraries hosted craft workshops and began lending tools to people. It is natural that libraries would host modern makerspaces, too. Libraries have always seen needs in societies and evolved to fulfill that need, particularly when it comes to helping the public access information and knowledge.

Recently, the Fayetteville Free Library in New York State became the first public library to create a modern makerspace in the United States, which it calls the Fabulous Laboratory, or "Fab Lab." The impetus for the idea came from a graduate student at Syracuse University. Lauren Britton Smedley wrote a paper about the possible use of makerspaces in libraries. On the Fayetteville library website, Smedley explained her thinking: "Public libraries exist to provide free and open access to information, technology and ideas. Building a makerspace . . . will provide our community with the opportunity to have free access to this world-changing technology." The executive director of the Fayetteville Free Library believed in Smedley's message and hired her to establish the makerspace. Today's Fayetteville Fab Lab boasts five 3-D (three-dimensional) printers, a vinyl cutter, sewing machines, jewelry making tools, knitting and crochet kits, and more.

CHAPTER TWO

THE BIG IDEA

Some people might wonder how the makers in a makerspace come up with an idea or project. Makers often need a little inspiration from others before they dive into creating for themselves. Most of these people are not copying others' ideas but finding out how they "think outside the box." Inspiration may come from walking around a makerspace and talking to makers, looking at online maker forums, or exploring a Maker Faire.

MAKER FAIRE

A Maker Faire is a gathering of makers of all ages and backgrounds for the purpose of showing their inventions and projects and sharing creative experiences. It is funded by Maker Media, the organization behind *Make* magazine. Maker Faires aim to spread ingenuity, enthusiasm for the maker movement, and new technologies.

The first Maker Faire took place in 2006. In 2012, 165,000 people attended Maker Faires in the cities of San Francisco and New York alone. According to the official Maker Faire website, nearly one hundred smaller community Maker Faires were held around the world the year of this writing. The number is expected to increase each year. Maker Faires are not just for users of makerspaces. They are for makers who create in their garages, bedrooms, and backyards. Maker Faires are especially for people who just want to be inspired to produce something of their own.

An attendee at a Maker Faire learns how ordinary household items can be turned into cat toys. Inventions can be complicated or simple like these.

ONLINE INSPIRATION

Thingiverse is an online community for makers to share their own 3-D printable creations and find out about others' designs. Rather than being worried about people stealing others' ideas, this community is encouraged to share ideas so that makers can learn from and improve on others' work.

Make magazine's website is also a good resource of inventiveness. Its project page offers ideas in categories such as electronics, crafts, home, and art. Each project is rated in difficulty, so there is something for both the beginner and the skilled to attempt.

INSPIRED INVENTORS

Many successful inventors have found that their best products were solutions to problems. For example, the inventor of the Leatherman multitool, Tim Leatherman, found himself wishing for pliers in a hotel room when he only had a pocketknife. When he figured out a way to combine those tools, he began a business that would grow into a multimillion-dollar enterprise.

The inventor of Velcro, George de Mestral, came up with his big idea, not with a problem, but just by noticing the natural world. He witnessed on a walk through the woods that burrs stuck to his pants and to his dog's fur. He thought a similar fastener could be useful in some way.

Makers repeatedly find themselves in similar situations as these two inventors: either something occurs to them, or they have a problem they need to fix. Either way, a makerspace often has what they need to make the idea into a reality.

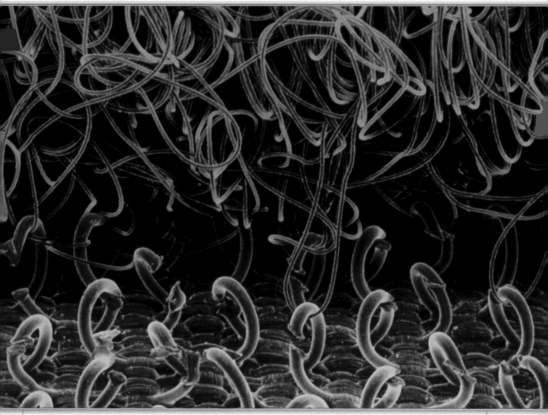

This close-up image of Velcro was captured with a scanning electron microscope. It shows how George de Mestral's invention works.

STOP AND THINK

People hoping to make a personal product in a makerspace should dive right in. However, makers focused on creating something profitable in the marketplace should stop and think.

In an interview with CNN.com, inventor and author Mike Bucci urged inventors to do research before beginning work on a product that they plan to take to market: "The best way to be successful as an inventor is always to educate yourself before taking action. I can't promise you'll get rich, but you'll certainly stand a much better chance of not going broke."

If the purpose of the product is to make money, makers need to ask themselves if there is a market for the product. In other words, do people need it or will they want to buy it? They should also question whether they are ready for the personal investment they will have to make. Inventors should expect to spend both time and money on their invention, and more of both than they think. Tim Leatherman warned in an interview with *Popular Mechanics*: "The time you devote will be double what you think it will be, and the dollar amounts you commit will be four times what you thought."

THE FIRST TO MARKET?

If a maker still wants to proceed with turning a concept into a profit-making product, he or she needs to find out if someone has already secured a patent for the idea. A patent is a property right granted by a government to an inventor to keep others from making or selling an invention throughout the country for a number of years. That invention becomes a person's intellectual property. Just as someone who buys land has the right to keep others off it, people can take measures to protect their intellectual property. Patents are only recognized in the country

PARTS OF THE PATENT

According to business publication Inc.com, there are four main tasks involved in filling out a patent application:

1. Describe an invention's background, including why it is different from other similar inventions and therefore deserves a patent.
2. Illustrate the invention through drawings, flowcharts, or diagrams. (Many inventors give this task to a graphic artist.)
3. Describe the invention's physical structure (if it has one) and how it works.
4. Describe what aspects of the invention should be patented.

in which they are granted, but inventors can apply for patents in other nations as well as their native country.

An introductory patent search is just a starting point. The U.S. Patent and Trademark Office has a searchable online database. If the idea is not in there, the inventor can proceed with submitting a provisional patent application, especially if he or she is worried about the idea being stolen. Other inventors wait and see if the concept pans out and then apply for a permanent patent.

Both patent applications cost money, sometimes several hundred dollars for the regular patent. After the application is filed, applicants will respond to questions and concerns from the patent office. They must prove that the idea or invention is truly unique. Receiving a patent is no guarantee that the product or invention will be a success, however. There is still a lot of hard work ahead.

The U.S. Patent and Trademark Office recommends that all patent applicants hire a patent attorney or patent agent to prepare their applications. Be aware that this is another added cost (perhaps several thousand dollars) to the cost of the regular patent application itself. However, it is not required, and many people do not hire an attorney.

CHAPTER THREE

SEARCHING FOR A SPACE

If a maker is lucky, he or she will have options when looking for a space. Makers may find what is needed in a commercial makerspace. The advantage of commercial makerspaces is that they aim to make a profit, and these profits can be used to buy the best equipment and pay a talented and available staff.

The drawback of a commercial makerspace is that using the facilities costs money. Makers, especially young makers,

People interested in becoming members of a makerspace can ask to speak with a representative or other members. This way, they can learn if the space is for them before buying a membership.

often do not have the funds needed to buy a membership to a commercial makerspace on top of the funds needed for their projects. Luckily, there are alternatives to for-profit makerspaces, and they are perfect for the beginning maker.

LOOK TO THE LIBRARIES

Those looking for a makerspace might want to check out what is new at their local public library. The Fayetteville Free Library was the first, but not the only, library to get on board with makerspaces. In fact, some librarians see makerspaces as the future of libraries and as a way to reinvent these institutions in a time when so many want to access electronic books via tablets, rather than browse aisles of bookshelves. As Professor Dave Lankes of Syracuse University stated in a presentation to New York librarians, "Imagine libraries are places to learn and create, not consume and check out." He urged his colleagues to use their imaginations when thinking of the future. He argued that libraries should be community spaces where people can access and share knowledge and inventiveness, which is part of the definition of a makerspace, too.

Recently, the Chicago Public Library became the first major urban library to open a makerspace at its Harold Washington Library Center. Called the Maker Lab, the space opened for a trial period with plans to evaluate whether the space is succeeding. Canadian libraries, too, are getting on board with the maker movement. The latest is a joint venture between the Ottawa Public Library and the U.S. Embassy called Imagine Space.

COMMUNITY CENTERS

There are also community centers that host makerspaces. Community centers are a logical fit for a makerspace because a community already knows them as a physical place to gather for activities. Community centers usually receive funds from governments for programs to better their neighborhoods. The funds could help pay for the expensive tools and materials needed just to get a makerspace started.

In fact, setting up a makerspace in a community center is a good way to introduce the concept to people who might not otherwise think of themselves as needing such a space. Offering classes such as basic woodworking, sewing, and robotics could attract many and act as an entry point to the world of making.

Sometimes what is inside the makerspace is not as important as who is inside and what they are hoping to accomplish. Makerspaces can also help at-risk communities come together. They have been known to transform whole communities.

CAMPUS SPACES

College and university makerspaces are not necessarily just for college students. For example, Case Western Reserve University in Cleveland, Ohio, has an "invention center" called ThinkBox that is open to the public and even hosts design competitions. In fact, it is constructing a 50,000-square-foot

Case Western Reserve University students consult each other about a project at their school's makerspace—ThinkBox. They welcome the opportunity to collaborate on ideas outside their classrooms and labs.

(5,645-square-meter) seven-story facility, that will be one of the largest university makerspaces in the world.

Other campus spaces are reserved just for student use. Makers hoping to attend a community college or university as a student might want to research whether the institution has a makerspace. (ThinkBox encourages high school

MAKING A COMMUNITY BETTER

The Mt. Elliott Makerspace of Detroit, Michigan, tries to provide a positive and safe environment for families. It seeks to help its members feel empowered in order to make better lives for themselves, as well as to better their community. What better way to feel empowered than to provide someone with the feeling that he or she could be an entrepreneur? Mt. Elliott provides the tools for fabrication, as well as guides members through the process of taking a product to market.

Young people at a library makerspace attend a soldering workshop. They are learning to join electrical components to a circuit board.

Artisan's Asylum in Somerville, Massachusetts, is not just a place where people tinker with inventions. Actual businesses are operating out of the space, a former envelope factory. According to Boston.com, Artisan's Asylum has housed forty to fifty small manufacturing businesses. These businesses raised about $300,000 through the Internet website Kickstarter, which could enable them to secure new spaces. They are helping bolster the manufacturing economy in Somerville.

students to intern at its facility, another way to experience a college makerspace.)

Young makers do not necessarily have to go to a makerspace—it might come to them! Stanford University in California has implemented a program called FabLab@School. The program's mission is to create makerspaces in schools by supplying equipment, suggesting activities, and preparing teachers to help facilitate the space.

CHAPTER FOUR

WHAT'S INSIDE

True community makerspaces invite people of all ages to participate—or at least to come in and see what others are doing so that they can consider becoming makers themselves. However, even these makerspaces have differences among them. Future inventors will want to investigate to find out if the makerspace has what they will need to complete their project.

Different makers need diverse kinds and combinations of resources to create. They might require materials such as cardboard, plastic, paint, metal, and wood. They may need mechanical components, such as gears, belts, and pulleys. They might want electrical parts, such as chips, wires, and circuit boards. Many makerspaces also have advanced technology.

TECH HEAVEN

Some tools, machines, and electronics can really make a maker's life easier. Many are also too expensive to purchase for personal use, which is another reason why a makerspace is useful. A community can share such tools. Here is some advanced technology that many makerspaces own to help makers achieve success:

- A 3-D printer makes 3-D objects. Depending on the project, it might be able to fabricate a part or actually create a prototype.
- A welding machine provides the power and heat to join together pieces of material, such as plastic and metal.

A man looks at an object created by a 3-D printer at the CES (Consumer Electronics Show) in Las Vegas, Nevada.

- A laser cutter uses a carbon dioxide laser to cut through plastic and other materials. It can also be used to engrave text on materials.
- A milling machine is used for cutting, planing, contouring, and drilling solid material.

- A plasma cutter creates plasma hot enough to cut through metals of varying thicknesses.
- A vinyl cutter uses a blade to cut thin materials such as vinyl, cloth, cardboard, and thin metals.
- CNC stands for "Computer Numeric Control." A CNC router can make complicated and intricate cuts in wood.
- A drill press enables greater accuracy in drilling holes.
- A metal lathe holds a piece of metal so that it can be turned and shaped by a sharp tool.
- An Arduino is a single board microcontroller and software that makes electronics easier to program.
- CAD stands for "computer-aided design. CAD software is used to create drawings or illustrations and either 2-D or 3-D models.

EXPERT NEEDED

The best makerspaces house not just these machinery, tools, and supplies but also instructors to teach makers how to use them properly. This way, the makers can operate the equipment in a proper and safe manner and create the best product possible.

Many makerspaces encourage makers to sign up for classes to learn about certain processes, such as creating computer programs. Some makerspaces require users to obtain training before using expensive or complicated tools, such as 3-D printers and vinyl cutters.

Some makerspaces even have mentors—people who will guide makers during the entire process of making, whether it takes a week or a year. Many makerspaces rely on volunteers to provide their expertise and time in this way.

THE CHALLENGES OF A MAKERSPACE

A lot of money is required to run a makerspace. The cost of space, tools, supplies, and manpower are all considerations. Even when a location is already available, such as at many libraries, costs are considerable. Some kinds of fabrication equipment can have daunting price tags—a color 3-D printer may cost $20,000! The price of manpower can run high as well. Both community makerspaces and library makerspaces have a hard time fitting such costs into their budgets.

The role of volunteers and philanthropy will become increasingly important in the future. Some makerspaces have already found a way to cut costs by partnering with local businesses. Businesses can get good publicity and advertising by providing skilled volunteers and needed equipment. Vocational programs and trade unions could also partner with nearby spaces in the future. They could supply the skilled workers needed to facilitate a successful makerspace.

PERFECT TIMING

The amount of access to a makerspace is also important to consider. Some makerspaces are only open during certain hours. For example, makerspaces in libraries are often only accessible when the library is open and often just part of that time. Part of the reason for that is the limited number of employees to monitor activities both in the library and the makerspace.

Other kinds of makerspaces may be open for most of the day, yet still require makers to sign up for specific times to use the space or certain machines and tools. That way, makers are not waiting in line to use the resources.

Some makerspaces allow people to drop in and tinker anytime, as long as someone else is present. Many offer twenty-four-hour access to paying members. These makers receive a key and can go in to work on their projects anytime, day or night. Makers should investigate to figure out what the space near them requires and whether that will help or hinder their creative process.

FOR A FEE

Not every makerspace is cost-free, even if it is located in a public library. Some makerspaces are free to use but charge for the use of certain materials, such as printer plastic, card stock, and adhesive vinyl.

Many makerspaces charge a monthly or yearly fee. For example, MakeIt Labs in Nashua, New Hampshire, requires

ShopBot

A maker uses a CNC router to trim a case for a circuit board. The computer-controlled machine makes precise cuts.

members to pay $40 per month. Another kind of membership at $75 a month allows members more privileges. However, MakeIt allows people who really want to join but cannot afford the fee to trade work hours at the makerspace for time in the lab.

CHAPTER FIVE

LET'S GET STARTED

Once the inventor has an idea and has found a suitable makerspace, it is time to begin making. This process is different for every maker and may vary for each project an inventor tackles. However, makers who plan on bringing their product to market might want to follow the lead of those who have found success in including certain steps in their process.

MODEL BEHAVIOR

Successful inventors recommend keeping a record book of activity that includes written notes and sketches of ideas. Notes can help an inventor remember an important thought or a half-formed idea. Sketches can aid investors in explaining their goals to someone at a makerspace so that person can help in figuring out the best way to help. Records can also help with obtaining a patent. Sometimes people apply for a patent on the same invention at the same time. Notebooks and journals can assist the patent office in figuring out who came up with the idea initially.

A sketch can only give an inventor a two-dimensional idea of his or her product. To get a better idea of the whole invention, makers might want to use CAD software that many makerspaces have. There are actually free programs available that can create 3-D objects onscreen, such as BRL-CAD and Blender. Makerspaces might have classes or one-on-one help for learning how to use this software.

Computer-aided design (CAD) software is used in many fields, including engineering and architecture. A makerspace can show inventors how CAD software can help them in their making process.

BUILDING THE PROTOTYPE

Even if an inventor has a vivid 3-D digital image of the product created by CAD software, he or she may still need an actual prototype of the invention to find out if it will work in the real world. The inventor might begin by creating the first prototype out of an available and easy-to-manipulate material, such as paper, to see how movable parts interact. This is a good way to

KEEPING IT CONFIDENTIAL

Inventors might wonder how to talk to others about their inventions without "giving their idea away." Many inventors worry about people stealing their ideas. That is why they get patents, so they can take legal action against intellectual property theft. However, many other inventors want to avoid the hassle and cost of acquiring a patent. What can they do?

As previously mentioned, inventors can file a provisional patent application to protect themselves. It is less money than a regular patent and will give the invention a "patent pending" status for at least a year. However, inventors can also have others sign a nondisclosure agreement, also called a confidentiality agreement. The agreement states what about the invention should be kept a secret and for how long.

Many inventors have these in hand when they meet with possible business partners. If someone refuses to sign a nondisclosure agreement, an inventor should take that as a warning sign and only proceed with extreme caution.

save time and money. Tim Leatherman, mentioned earlier as the inventor of the Leatherman multitool, built prototypes of his popular gadget from cardboard, wood, and metal until he finally decided on a design.

A 3-D printer could also come in handy at this point. It might be able to make a prototype of the whole product or just a single part. People have printed objects such as eyeglass frames, musical instruments, tools, toy cars, and more on a 3-D printer. These are not just models of objects—they actually work.

Some inventors without a makerspace may hire others to fabricate their inventions if they do not have the materials or machinery needed. Hiring others is an option, but it can be a very expensive decision. Luckily, many makerspaces have a variety of materials as well as the professional machinery needed to work with the materials.

As an inventor makes the actual prototype of the invention, he or she should keep track of the materials, supplies, and tools used and the exact steps taken to create it. The inventor will need to repeat these steps to make the product again and need to know how much money and time to expect to invest.

TROUBLESHOOTING

Problems often pop up in the process of making an invention come to life. Inventors may have to try using different materials, reworking the original design, or altering something else to make their product work. Feedback from others who know more about materials, electronics, or machinery can really come in handy at this point. Makerspaces usually have a few

An inventor displays the many materials and tools available at a workbench in a makerspace in Halifax, Nova Scotia, in Canada.

experienced makers around to give pointers. Also, inventors should not underestimate asking family and friends to offer constructive criticism about the product.

Inventors must remember that great inventions can take years to come to fruition. Tim Leatherman worked three years to create his multitool, and George de Mestral took eight years to perfect Velcro. It is really important to believe in the product and be unafraid of starting over when needed. Many people go into a makerspace with an idea for one project and end up with something completely different. True inventors are always ready to make a change and adapt to come up with something truly useful.

CHAPTER SIX

AFTER THE SPACE

O nce a maker has perfected the unique product that he or she thinks could be successful in the business world, it is time to consider how to bring it to market. The first thing to know is that there is not one correct route to follow. But that does not mean the route is not important. In fact, sometimes the path an inventor chooses to take is as important—or more so—than the product itself. The inventor should carefully consider the available options and not rush into a decision.

DO YOUR HOMEWORK

An online article for *Entrepreneur* magazine recommended several steps to get an invention to market. First, inventors should research as much as they can to figure out which market might be best for their product. For example, a guitar case with a holder for sheet music should be sold to music stores or at least places where musicians shop. Similarly, a smartphone case that holds lipstick would not be sold to a store that primarily carries goods for men.

The article also suggested finding similar products on the market. This is another way to identify possible companies that would be interested in selling the inventor's product. Inventors should investigate companies to be sure that they are reputable—for example, if they have a good rating with

Some magazines are geared toward entrepreneurs. Look for them at a local library. They can give up-to-date advice about jumping into the business world.

the Better Business Bureau (BBB)or if another inventor has had a positive interaction with them.

Other inventors are a valuable source of information. They can share their experiences and connect fellow inventors with professionals and invention-friendly businesses.

While an inventor may meet people like this at a maker-space, there are also associations for inventors, such as the United Inventors Organization of America. This is a national organization, but there are also state chapters of this group, which is dedicated to the support of inventors.

Inventors who do not have a business plan are taking a big risk that their inventions—no matter how in demand or clever—will not take off in the marketplace.

PICK A PLAN

Will the inventor start a business to create his or her product?
Sometimes a business plan can help him or her make the most
sensible choice. A business plan is a written statement about
an inventor's goals for the product and the means for achieving
these goals. A basic business plan has four parts: a description
of the business, a plan for marketing the product, a strategy for
securing and spending money for production, and a proposal for
managing the business. By creating this plan, the inventor will
get an estimate of the financial reality of producing a product and
running a business.

Now the inventor can decide if he or she will try to raise
the money needed to accomplish this or license the product
to an already existing business. Licensing is the process of
selling an idea to a company that will take on all the tasks
that launching a new product involves. The drawback of
licensing is that the inventor will only receive a small percentage of the profits. According to an article on CNN.com,
a realistic share for an inventor licensing a product is about 5
percent. Still, if the product flies off the shelves, the inventor
might be rewarded well by choosing licensing.

SELL SHEETS

Many inventors hoping to license their products create sell
sheets. These are one-page descriptions of the product that are

MORE FOR MAKERS AT THE LIBRARY

Not only do public libraries host some of the most accessible makerspaces, but they are also a great place to learn how to evaluate an invention's market-ability. There is a nationwide network of libraries that work with the U.S. Patent and Trademark Office to provide invention information to the public. About eighty Patent and Trademark Resource Centers across the United States are open to inventors to research patents, investigate ways to go to market with a product, and talk to professionals about concerns. Many Patent and Trademark Resource Centers provide free, one-on-one consultations as well as large group trainings.

sent by mail or e-mail or distributed in face-to-face meetings to businesses or other parties. The sell sheet is meant to attract attention to the product and excite a possible business partner into wanting to produce the product. It should:

- Describe the product's uses, functions, and benefits
- Pinpoint the product's markets
- Highlight the product's unique and exciting nature
- Have multiple color photographs of the product

- Include the legal status of the product (for example, patent pending or copyright information)

If the sell sheet is not presented face to face, an accompanying letter should introduce the inventor and explain why he or she has chosen to contact that company. The inventor should follow up by calling and requesting a meeting with the business.

Some people recommend contacting at least fifty companies about the product, knowing that most will not make an offer. Inventors can make a list of possible companies by researching Internet business databases. Industry trade shows are also a good place to meet interested parties. Check the Internet for information about local meetings.

Above all, inventors should not get discouraged in the process of getting their product to market. Not receiving offers from businesses about an invention is not necessarily a reflection on the product. Companies are approached with new products all the time; sometimes great ideas slip through the cracks.

CHAPTER SEVEN

RAISING CAPITAL

So what if an inventor decides to become an entrepreneur? What if he or she wants to create a business but does not have the requisite funds? Fortunately, there are ways of getting the money needed to get a project off the ground. In fact, there are more ways than ever before, thanks to the Internet. The process of obtaining funds for a business venture is called raising capital.

CAPITALISTS, ANGELS, GRANTS

Investors called venture capitalists provide funds for inventions or businesses if they believe that the investment will be profitable in the future. These investors usually work for a venture capital firm and invest money out of a general fund. Inventors can research venture capital firms online to find which are more likely to give money for "early stage" investments. They should consider the organization's location and experience in the relevant market. Venture capital is typically the hardest money to get because the investors need a lot of convincing.

Angel investors are another possibility for raising capital. These are people with spare funds and some personal or business-related interest. They could be wealthy relatives or a local business owner who believes in the product. According to the *Harvard Business Review*, angel investors

Venture capitalists such as these who invested $200 million in Apple-related products, offer money for businesses they believe will yield profits.

recently supplied more than $22 billion to about 65,000 companies, while venture capitalists invested about $28 billion in about 3,700 companies. A well-written business plan is a must when contacting both venture capitalists and angel investors, as most will ask to review it before taking a chance.

In addition to these sources, both private businesses and governments offer grants for inventions. Grants.gov is a helpful online source to check for grants from the federal government. Inventors' organizations often have good sources for other kinds of grants. Some grants are only awarded for certain kinds of inventions. For example, an invention that will help cut down the use of fossil fuels might receive a grant from an environmental organization. Some grants are especially for young inventors. The National Collegiate Inventors and Innovators Alliance (NCIIA) offers grants to college students who are inventors.

CROWDFUNDING

Crowdsourcing is the practice of obtaining services or ideas by soliciting contributions from a large group of people and especially from the online community. Crowdsourcing is increasingly becoming a popular way for people to raise the capital they need for different projects. This is called crowdfunding.

Musicians have used crowdfunding to raise money to make albums or go on tour. Actors and directors have raised money to produce movies. Makers, too, can use crowdfunding to get the money they need to start a business. According to Entrepreneur.com, there are more than six hundred crowdfunding sources online. Here are some of the most popular.

Kickstarter (www.kickstarter.com) is one of the most popular and well-known crowdfunding sites. The site even makes it possible to support local projects and products that need funding.

KICKSTARTER

Since 2009, Kickstarter has helped fund nearly fifty thousand creative projects with pledges of $843 million, according to its website. Filmmakers, musicians, artists, and designers have all found success here. Those asking for funding often promise contributors something in return, such as the ability to pre-order the finished product. According to an ABCNews.com article, a product called the Pebble Smartwatch raised $10 million on Kickstarter.

Funding on Kickstarter is all-or-nothing, which means that projects must reach their funding goals to receive any money. In addition, there is a 5 percent fee charged

Shown here from left to right are Ben Kaufman, founder of the crowdfunding site Quirky, and Jake Zien, inventor of the Pivot Power adjustable power strip.

for services. People can browse Kickstarter projects at www.kickstarter.com.

INDIEGOGO

Indiegogo began as a crowdfunding source for the independent movie industry. However, in 2009, it expanded to all areas of industry and business. According to its website, Indiegogo is the leading international crowdfunding source. Top campaigns have earned millions of dollars each, usually for technological inventions hoping to go to market.

There is a fee on money raised, 4 percent of the total if the goal is met or 9 percent if the goal is not met. Indiegogo does not place restrictions on project creators. Anyone with an idea, a financial need, and a bank account may create a campaign. Inventors can check it out at www .indiegogo.com.

QUIRKY

Quirky is a site geared toward inventors, but with a twist. Quirky users can start the process with an idea and allow others to vote on whether it is worthwhile. Any of Quirky's community members can offer opinions on how to improve or tweak the product. However, it is the Quirky organization that designs, manufactures, and sells the product if it is deemed valuable. Inventors who submit accepted ideas and "influencers" who contribute to the ideas share in royalties based on product sales. Quirky ultimately holds

JAKE ZIEN, QUIRKY INVENTOR

Jake Zien was a student at the Rhode Island School of Design with an idea: a power strip that could flex around furniture and accommodate large adapters in each outlet. However, as a college student, Zien had few resources to take his idea to market. After consulting with an intellectual property lawyer and discovering that a patent for his idea could cost close to $10,000, he discovered Quirky. The Quirky community got behind his idea. The Quirky engineers prototyped the piece with a 3-D printer and set up manufacturing in China. Today anyone can buy Zien's Pivot Power strip. Jake has earned more than $400,000 for his idea so far, according to his Quirky online profile.

the patent, though. Some of Quirky's products are found in major stores such as Target, Amazon.com, and Bed, Bath, and Beyond. Investigate Quirky at www.quirky.com.

CHAPTER EIGHT

MAKERSPACE MAKERS

Though the makerspace movement is still relatively new and growing in momentum, many people with an idea and the dream of inventing the next big thing may find that they do not have a makerspace in their community. Some of these people are deciding to open their own makerspaces. How do they do this?

STARTING FROM SCRATCH

A makerspace requires a great deal of money just to get started. Consider the finances needed to buy or rent a space, purchase equipment, pay staff, and acquire the necessary permits, licenses, and insurance. According to *Make* magazine, it may cost $1.5 million to start a makerspace, even one with a monthly membership fee. No matter how they plan to get the money, makerspace organizers need to plan a budget. Some seek donations, sponsorships from businesses, and government grants. Others use online crowdfunding sites. Sometimes the promise of merchandise from makerspace members entices donors. Even if funds are secured, there is still a lot of work to do to attract members and keep the space working.

People interested in having a makerspace in their community might do best to contact their local library about starting one. They should have a proposal ready for library management, including information about how other libraries have started

Finding a physical space is just one of many steps in creating the perfect makerspace. It takes many people to create a successful workspace for makers and many to keep it functioning.

makerspaces. The proposal should also contain research about how the makerspace might benefit both the library and the community around it.

THE FUTURE OF MAKERSPACES

In the future, people may not have to go to a community center or library to find a makerspace that fits them. Makers might not even need a physical space at all. They may be able to find a virtual space online that offers what they need. Of course, they

DETERMINED SCIENTIST

Sixteen-year-old Katriona Guthrie-Honea of Seattle, Washington, had a problem. She made a model of a biosensor, a device that monitors and transmits information about certain genes. Her model was so inventive that she won a prize at the Northwest Association for Biomedical Research Student Biotech Expo. However, Guthrie-Honea wanted to continue working on her research. She tried to find a biotech lab to work in but was turned down for being too young. She got lucky: she was granted an internship at a cancer research center. However, her experience made her realize that young people were often helpless to pursue an idea, especially in the biotech industry.

In a GeekWire interview, Guthrie-Honea said: "I was really, really motivated to find a place to work, but what about people that have a small idea and kind of want to test it out? They're going to get turned away, right away." So Guthrie-Honea and a partner decided to create Seattle's first biotech makerspace, a place for anyone—teens and adults—to test out their scientific endeavors. They raised the money for their venture on Microryza, a crowdfunding site geared toward science. They exceeded their goal, and now their HiveBio Community Lab is up and running. HiveBio charges a drop-in fee to cover rent, but members can also buy unlimited access to the lab and classes.

would not be able to make use of all the tools, machines, and other resources that today's makerspaces have. Perhaps, in addition to online makerspaces, roving makerspaces could travel to different communities to share tools and expertise, somewhat like some libraries have bookmobiles.

Online makerspaces might take the form of video chats, either one-on-one or an instructor with a number of students. In fact, there are already some online maker services available. The

A future maker plays with an interactive music-video program at a Maker Faire in San Mateo, California. Exhibitions are important for promoting the various kinds of products that can be created in makerspaces.

Make to Learn Design Center, at www.maketolearn.org, is one. It provides an online space where teachers and students come together virtually to learn about digital fabrication.

By going online, makers could tap into the expansive knowledge of people from all over the globe to learn about fabrication processes. Multiple makerspaces around the globe could be linked for widespread collaboration. This might solve some of the obstacles that makerspaces face: inadequate finances to hire staff and a limited pool of professionals who can share expertise.

There is another bonus of digitally connected makerspaces for aspiring entrepreneurs. Employers, investors, and savvy business-people might take an interest in them and look for new products to take to market that way. This would take some of the pressure off makers hoping to find connections in the business world.

A SPACE IS WAITING

Many makerspaces host special events for people to drop by and check out the atmosphere, investigate the kinds of tools available, and see the various projects that makers are working on. If you pop into a makerspace, be sure to strike up a conversation with makers and ask them about their experiences.

No matter what you are is interested in—biotechnology, electronics, mechanics, fashion, or something else—a makerspace is out there for you. Besides a makerspace's material benefits, perhaps its most important contribution is providing opportunity. Few places offer so many the chance to learn and create. Undoubtedly, in the future, more successful inventors will get their start in their community's makerspace.

board A group of people chosen to make decisions.

capital Money, usually used to launch a business.

CNC machining A process used in manufacturing that involves the use of computers to control machine tools.

commercial Relating to buying and selling goods or services.

contour To shape one thing so that it fits the outlines of another.

fabrication The construction or the process of building.

grant A sum of money given by a government or organization to fund a project or initiative.

impetus Something that provides energy or motivation to accomplish something.

ingenuity Cleverness or originality.

license Official permission granted by an authority.

marketability Being in demand and easy to sell.

microcontroller An integrated circuit that controls some or all of the functions of an electronic device or system.

nondisclosure agreement An agreement to not discuss certain information.

philanthropy A desire to improve the world through activities.

plane To use a device to smooth or shape the surface of wood.

prototype A functioning model having the same features of later forms.

provisional Temporary or conditional.

router A tool that cuts grooves and hollows in wood and other materials.

royalty A percentage of the income from an invention's income that is paid to the inventor.

solicit To try to get something by making frequent requests.

trade union An organization of workers formed to protect the rights and interests of its members.

Canadian Intellectual Property Office (CIPO)
Place du Portage I
50 Victoria Street, Room C-114
Gatineau, K1A 0C9
Canada
(866) 997-1936
Website: http://www.cipo.ic.gc.ca
Find out what is needed to obtain a patent, trademark, or copyright in Canada and to protect intellectual property.

Fayetteville Free Library Fab Lab
300 Orchard Street
Fayetteville, NY 13066
(315) 637-6374
Website: http://www.fflib.org/fablab
As the first library in the United States to host a makerspace, Fayetteville Free Library continues to update and promote its Fab Lab for the local maker community.

HiveBio
Building G Talaris Center
4000 NE 41st Street
Seattle, WA 98105
E-mail: HiveBio@gmail.com
Website: http://hivebio.org
The HiveBio is the community-supported makerspace biology laboratory located in Seattle, Washington, and begun by sixteen-year-old Katriona Guthrie-Honea.

Think Haus
25 Dundurn Street North
Hamilton, ON L8R 3C9
Canada
E-mail: mailadmin@thinkhaus.org
Website: http://www.thinkhaus.org
This is a place for "hackers, makers, crafters, and artists" to share, learn, and work on projects together in Hamilton, Ontario.

U.S. Patent and Trademark Office
Director of the U.S. Patent and Trademark Office
P.O. Box 1450
Alexandria, VA 22313-1450
(800) 786-9199
Website: http://www.uspto.gov
This organization is an agency of the U.S. Department of Commerce. It is dedicated to helping people in the United States protect their intellectual property.

WEBSITES

Due to the changing nature of Internet links, Rosen Publishing has developed an online list of websites related to the subject of this book. This site is updated regularly. Please use this link to access the list:

http://www.rosenlinks.com/MAKER/Idea

Baichtal, John. *Hack This: 24 Incredible Hackerspace Projects from the DIY Movement.* Indianapolis, IN: Que, 2012.

Bender, Lionel. *Invention.* New York, NY: DK Publishing, 2013.

Clark, Brenda. *Entrepreneurship.* Tinley Park, IL: Goodheart-Willcox, 2013.

Evans, Brian. *Practical 3D Printers.* New York, NY: Apress, 2012.

Ferguson Publishing. *Careers in Focus: Entrepreneurs.* New York, NY: Ferguson, 2009.

Frauenfelder, Mark. *Make: Technology on Your Time.* Sebastopol, CA: Dale Dougherty/O'Reilly Media, 2005.

Kemp, Adam. *The Makerspace Workbench: Tools, Technologies, and Techniques for Making.* Sebastopol, CA: Maker Media, 2013.

Kennedy, Joseph Paul, et. al. *How to Invent and Protect Your Invention: A Guide to Patents for Scientists and Engineers.* Hoboken, NJ: Wiley, 2012.

Lawton, Kevin, and Dan Marom. *The Crowdfunding Revolution: How to Raise Venture Capital Using Social Media.* New York, NY: McGraw-Hill, 2013.

Lipson, Hod, and Melba Kurman. *Fabricated: The New World of 3D Printing.* Hoboken, NJ: Wiley, 2013.

Preddy, Leslie. *School Library Makerspaces: Grades 6-12.* Santa Barbara, CA: Libraries Unlimited, 2013.

Roslund, Samantha, and Emily Puckett Rodgers. *Makerspaces.* Ann Arbor, MI: Cherry Lake Publishing, 2014.

Bagley, Caitlyn. "What Is a Makerspace? Creativity in the Library." *ALA TechSource*, December 20, 2012. Retrieved October 31, 2013 (http://www.alatechsource.org).

Balle, Louise. "What Is a Product Sell Sheet?" Chron.com. Retrieved November 18, 2013 (http://smallbusiness .chron.com/product-sell-sheet-23659.html).

Barnett, Chance. "Top 10 Crowdfunding Sites for Fundraising." *Forbes*, May 8, 2013. Retrieved September 30, 2013 (http:// www.forbes.com/sites/chancebarnett/2013/2-13/05/08/ top-10-crowdfunding-sites-for-funding).

Bellis, Mary. "Making a Prototype." About.com. Retrieved November 11, 2013 (http://inventors.about.com/od/ prototypes/a/prototype.htm).

Borland, John. "Hacker Space Movement Sought for U.S." Wired.com, August 11, 2007. Retrieved September 30, 2013 (http://www.wired.com/threatlevel/2007/08/us -hackers-moun).

Brady-Brown, Annabel, and Ane Feier Knudsen. "A Visit to the Mothership." Exberliner.com, October 17, 2012. Retrieved November 14, 2013 (http://www.exberliner.com/features/ lifestyle/a-visit-to-the-mothership).

Breitkopf, Mia. "A Makerspace Takes Over a Local Library." Syracuse University, December 1, 2011. Retrieved November 2, 2013 (http://infospace.ischool.syr.edu/2011 /12/01/a-makerspace-takes-over-a-local-library).

Calvanti, Gui. "Is It a Hackerspace, Makerspace, TechShop, or FabLab?" *Make*, May 22, 2013. Retrieved November 22, 2013 (http://makezine.com/2013/05/22/the-difference -between-hackerspaces-makerspaces-techshops-and -fablabs).

Educause. "7 Things You Should Know About Makerspaces." Educause.edu, April 2013. Retrieved November 2, 2013 (www.educause.edu/ir/library/pdf/ELI7095.pdf).

Gorman, Jim. "How to Become an Inventor (in 5 Steps). *Popular Mechanics*, July 26, 2010. Retrieved October 20, 2013 (http://www.popularmechanics.com/technology/engineering/gonzo/how-to-become-an-inventor-in-5-steps-2).

Gorman, Jim. "How to File a Patent for Your Invention." *Popular Mechanics*, July 26, 2010. Retrieved October 28, 2013 (http://www.popularmechanics.com).

Inc.com. "Can You Get a Patent Without a Lawyer?" Inc.com. Retrieved October 20, 2013 (http://www.forbes.com/sites/tjmccue/2011/11/15/first-public-library-to-create-a-maker-space).

McCue, TJ. "First Public Library to Create a Makerspace." Forbes.com, November 15, 2011. Retrieved October 15, 2013 (https://www.adafruit.com/blog/2012/11/12/how-to-start-a-hackerspace/).

Makerfair.com. "Maker Faire." Maker Media. Retrieved November 23, 2013 (http://makerfaire.com/makerfairehistory).

Michaud, Eric. "How to Start a Hackerspace." Adafruit Learning System. Retrieved November 14, 2013 (http://learn.adafruit.com).

Suddath, Claire. "A Brief History of: Velcro." *Time*, June 15, 2010. Retrieved November 5, 2013 (http://content.time.com/time/nation/article/0,8599,1996883,00.html).

ABOUT THE AUTHOR

Therese Shea, an author and former educator, has written over one hundred books on a wide variety of subjects. Her most recent have delved into hot topics in technology, including Lego Mindstorms programming, robotics clubs, gamification, and a biography of innovator and Apple cofounder Steve Jobs. She holds degrees from Providence College and the State University of New York at Buffalo. The author currently resides in Rochester, New York, with her husband, Mark.

PHOTO CREDITS

Cover, pp. 1, 4-5, 25 Mitch Altman; pp. 7, 14, 21, 27, 33, 39, 45, 52 © iStockphoto.com/Tommounsey; p. 8 Sergei Bachlakov/Xinhua/Landov; p. 10 Matt Stamey/Gainesville Sun/Landov; p. 15 Jason DeCrow/ Invision for Purina ONE/AP images; p. 17 Breger Dee/Photo Researchers/Getty Images; p. 21 (inset) © Jeff Janowski/The Augusta Chronicle/ZUMA Press; pp. 24, 32 Gus Chan/The Plain Dealer/ Landov; p. 28 Britta Pedersen/DPA/Landov; p. 34 © Gary Conner/ PhotoEdit; pp. 37, 46 © AP Images; p. 40 © Michael Newman/ PhotoEdit; p. 41 Didecs/Shutterstock.com; p. 48 © iStockphoto.com/ SeanShot; p. 50 Sundance Channel, Christian Clothier/AP Images; p. 53 Jupiterimages/Stockbyte/Thinkstock; p. 55 Kimberly White/ Reuters/Landov; cover and interior page design elements © iStockphoto.com/Samarskaya (cover wires), © iStockphoto.com/klenger (interior wires), © iStockphoto.com/A-Digit (circuit board design), © iStockphoto.com/Steven van Soldt (metal plate), © iStockphoto.com/Storman (background pp. 4-5).